Body Language

Master Body Language &

Non-Verbal Communication

For Increased Influence In

Relationships & At Work

Steve Gold

Table of Contents

Conclusion

A message from the author, Steve Gold

<u>Introduction</u>

Have you ever wished you could read other people's minds? Wished you could be like Sherlock Holmes who could tell so much about people he'd just met from seemingly insignificant clues, such as their clothing, perfume, accessories or the lint on their jackets? Wouldn't it be amazing to have that ability?

Understanding body language gives you a similar ability. By watching other people's gestures, expressions, and movements, you will be able to decipher what a person is *really* thinking or saying. Through millions of years or evolution and survival, we have developed ways of expressing thoughts and emotions apart from the use of words. It is so knitted into who we are that we are hardly even aware of our bodies' non-verbal communication. However, this communication is always there if you know how to look for it.

Have you ever met a person for the first time and felt distrust without knowing why? Or, maybe you've met someone you instantly felt comfortable with even though you'd just met? You may not know it, but you were most likely picking up signals from the other person's body language and were evaluating them subconsciously.

Learning about body language will help you understand your own feelings as well as your reactions towards others. It can also help you understand other people much more thoroughly, by not only listening to their words but by also reading their unspoken cues. Think of the possibilities! Is your date interested in you? How can you make a more powerful impact at work?

Reading body language is an innate ability that we all have and, as mentioned, to some degree use unconsciously. In this book, we'll look at how to take your reading of body language from something you do unconsciously to something you are conscious of. As you begin to learn this invaluable skill, you'll see just how useful it can be in all areas of your life!

Chapter 1

Evolution and Body Language

The purpose of body language

Non-verbal language had existed millions of years, since long before man started communicating using words. In the past, man used grunts, groans and gestures to communicate. Despite the fact that the human race has come a long way through civilization, science and technology, our original method of communication is still very much in use. Body language is undoubtedly our first language. The "no" gesture of moving the face from side to side is said to have originated from the breastfeeding baby refusing its mother's milk. Satiated, perhaps, or simply not hungry, the infant moves its head from side to side, avoiding its mother's breast.

Charles Darwin himself was the first to formally study body language. He recorded his thoughts and findings in his book titled, "The Expression of the Emotions in Man and Animals" which he published in 1872. Later, during the era of silent movies, actors began to study how people expressed emotions through their bodies. The 60s was when serious studies were conducted by experts on behavior.

Kinesics is the study of body language. It aims to establish the meaning of our gestures and their origins. Although body language does not involve grammar or syntax, it is popularly referred to as a language because gestures do express thoughts.

Usually, even before speaking a word, people who meet you for the first time have already formed their impression of who you are based on your body language. Reading body language is tricky and subject to a variety of interpretations. Thus, one must know how to read non-verbal signals correctly in order to avoid misunderstanding and conflict.

Verbal communication is mainly used to put across ideas and facts while body language is what communicates feelings. Nowadays, it is possible to communicate without seeing or hearing a person; but by simply using words or typing text messages. This, however, has caused some of us lose touch with accurately reading non-verbal language. On the other hand, non-verbal communication has never been more significant, as people can influence others through videos on the internet; sending signals and exploiting the tools available in the form of visual media.

So, while in the past, gestures were developed for survival in primitive societies, learning and understanding body language is still valuable today in order to enhance relationships, improve one's career prospects, become more empowered, communicate beliefs efficiently and even to escape possible harm.

Why women tend to be more intuitive

We've all heard of "women's intuition" and you've most likely encountered it first-hand. How did your mom know you were lying? How did your wife know you'd been cheating?

Experts have established through studies that women do have the upper hand in reading non-verbal cues. It was also noted to be especially true for mothers. The reason may be that, while raising a child, women spend the infant's early years trying to understand a small human who cannot speak, and whose only form of communication is through crying, flailing of arms, clenching their fists, kicking their legs or making a thousand different facial expressions. It's no surprise, therefore that women have learned to make meaning of these movements in order to understand. Also, from an evolutionary point of view, women may have better developed intuitive skills because they tend not to be as strong or because they were encumbered by having to watch their children; so they made up for this by developing better observation and better body language interpretation skills. This helped them to have a better chance of escaping danger or serious threats to their lives.

Research using Magnetic Resonance Imaging (MRI) has also shown that women have more areas in the brain than men associated with interpreting non-verbal cues. To this day, women have retained this ancient instinct and, although the world is no longer as dangerous as is was during ancient times, this special ability can still come in quite handy.

Children are more transparent

As discussed, mothers get a lot of practice in reading body language when raising children as children are easy to read due to the fact that their actions are obvious and undisguised. An angry toddler will stomp her foot, scowl and utter a loud "Hmmph!" Adults have learned the art of subtlety and pretense. Perhaps, instead of stomping his foot, a man would discretely tap his finger on the tabletop. Instead of a full scowl, he'd purse his lips and try to form a crooked smile. The "hmmph" would be toned down to a "hmm," but the same emotion is there nonetheless. Pressure from society has taught adults to suppress their emotions and to try to hide or disguise their body language. Indeed, learning to tone down one's non-verbal messaging can be useful especially in avoiding unnecessary conflict and confrontation.

It is interesting to note that studies have proven that even children with autism are able to read a person's emotions from the body language they exhibit. Body language is a useful tool for parents and teachers in helping a child grow up to be empathetic and confident.

How to read body language

So is it possible to accurately read a person's mind from his or her body language?

To that, the answer would be both yes and no. Learning to read people is a very powerful and useful tool. But we also have to avoid the mistake of judging people unfairly or giving the wrong meaning to their actions. Here's how we do this:

1. Be observant

Watch people. Note their facial expressions, arm movements, distance from you, posture, voice, etc. Try to figure out what's going on and how they're feeling. You may not know if your guesses are correct, but your skill in observation will improve. This will improve your understanding of as well as your interaction with others.

2. Learn the language

This is where this book comes in. Be aware of the meanings of certain gestures and facial expressions. Of course, no one book can cover all the possible gestures or expressions we are capable of making, but knowing the basics will put you on the right track.

3. Practice, practice, practice!

No one can be an instant expert on body language. Try watching videos (that you've never watched before) with the audio on mute and try to guess what's going on, what the situation is in the scene. Write down the emotions you feel are being acted out and which gestures gave you that clue. Play the video again, this time with the sound on and see how accurate your reading of the situation was.

You can also simply watch old silent movies and note how the actors express the feelings of the characters. These movies are the perfect way to start to become more conscious of body language as silent movie actors were some of the first people to think seriously about the importance of body language.

You could also practice by observing a friend, colleague or someone you have just met and tactfully asking if your interpretation of their mood or occupation is correct. I once had a hunch that the person I was talking to was a teacher because of the way she spoke and her eagerness to share information. I asked her and found out I was right. It felt good to know I was learning to pick up unspoken cues from other people.

4. Consider the context

Age, culture, physical health, environment, gender – all of these can influence a person's body language. A person may be releasing deep sighs not because he's frustrated with you but because he has a cold and finds it difficult to breathe. She's not scratching her head because she's confused, it may simply be because of dandruff. He's not crossing his arms in defiance; he's simply feeling cold.

To avoid making an unjust interpretation of the other person's non-verbal language, it's important to see the whole picture.

5. Find as many instances as possible

Observation must be validated by other instances. Before writing someone off as a liar based on just one instance, make more observations. A liar will oftentimes consistently lie, and this will show in many ways, many times, not just once.

6. Balance the verbal with the non-verbal

What is being said should be consistent with what the body is signaling. When a person is bluffing, his body language will give him away. Some people, such as politicians, actors and salespeople, are adept at faking their body language. They have carefully studied how to appear friendly and convincing. But faking cannot be maintained for extended periods of time, and their genuine convictions will eventually be reflected in their gestures and mannerisms.

Why learn to read body language?

1. It enhances communication- you will learn to better read between the lines and understand

the speaker's *actual* message. Moreover, you will also learn to convey your feelings and ideas even more efficiently using body language.

2. It makes you more understanding and sympathetic- being aware of body signals will help you anticipate other people's needs and understand their difficulties. You will understand what they are unable to articulate.

3. It will make you less vulnerable – you will be aware if a person is trying to manipulate, deceive or hurt you and you will be better prepared react or resist.

4. It will make you a better person- understanding others will lead to understanding yourself as well, and this in turn, can lead to establishing and maintaining more stable relationships. It can be valuable, not only in one's personal life, but in one's career as well.

Chapter 2

How the Body Speaks

Body language is not a lost art. We "speak" it unknowingly all the time. Now, it's time to learn to use this language to our advantage. To do so requires that we understand it first. Let's look at the different ways by which we communicate our feelings and ideas through body language.

Personal space

Personal space is that invisible extension or air around us that we consider our own. It is not a part of our body, but we claim it as our territory. The size of our personal space is largely influenced by the environment in which we were raised. People who grew up accustomed to vast open spaces and a sparse population have a bigger personal space. This means that they are not very comfortable having people coming too close to them. Those who are used to crowds and smaller living spaces have a smaller personal space. They don't mind as much when people, especially strangers, are in close proximity

Usually, people have an intimate space where only a chosen few are allowed to enter. It is reserved for close friends, family or lovers. Pets are also allowed because they are not seen as a threat. An unwelcome "intruder" will be resented or rejected, sometimes aggressively.

It is important to be sensitive to how close a person will allow you to stand next to them. This space that you are authorized to occupy varies from culture to culture, gender to gender and individual to individual. In general, one's personal space is guarded closely, and it is best not to trespass within these boundaries. Invasion of one's personal space explains why aggression can quickly break out in a crowd and why the crowd has to be dispersed before the tension will ease.

Road rage can also be a result of perceived invasion into one's territory (in which a person includes his car and the space around it as his). Persons of opposite gender entering the other's intimate zone may be perceived as making sexual advances. Sometimes, in instances where an invasion of space is unavoidable, such as in the subway or elevator, people cope by shutting themselves out – not talking and having a blank expression, for example. The main thing to remember is simply to keep your distance. When dealing with people who are used to wide open spaces and a large personal space, perhaps a greeting from a distance will be better than a handshake. Remember that a person's personal space is his "sacred space" and you are to respect that until you are allowed to enter it.

Posture

There's a good reason our parents always told us to stand or sit up straight. A sloucher looks weak and submissive while the person with good posture looks confident and powerful. This is well within reason. When we slouch, we restrict the flow of oxygen to our lungs, and we make ourselves appear smaller. This kind of posture puts unnecessary strain on our neck and back muscles. Overall, it strains our body, reduces the flow of energy in our body and makes us look unattractive. What do we do when we are exhausted and ready to give up? We slouch. To overcome slouching, one needs to strengthen the back and torso by exercising (yoga is helpful) as well as by staying mindful of and practicing good posture until it becomes a habit.

A healthy diet will also help strengthen your bones and muscles as well as give you a more positive outlook on life. If it does not come naturally to you, you'll have to make an extra effort to improve your posture. It may be a little difficult, but it's not impossible, and it will definitely be worth the effort.

The face and head

The face is always a dead giveaway when we try to hide our true feelings. All parts of the face - eyebrows, nose, mouth, eyes- interact to give others a clear indication of our true feelings.

Let's start with the whole head. When the head is positioned upright and remains still during a conversation, it shows neutrality. But when it is lifted high with the chin jutting out, this shows defiance, arrogance, aggression or the feeling of superiority. By lifting the chin, the neck is exposed. The person lifts his head to appear taller and looks down condescendingly at you.

The opposite of chin-jutting might be the head tilt. As a person tilts his head to the side, he exposes his neck and makes himself look smaller. This signals submission and non-aggression. Many advertisements use this pose because we unconsciously recognize it as a signal of submission. Models using the head-tilt pose are perceived as attractive and likable.

If a person looks down while listening, he may disapprove or he may be critical of what you are saying. This applies in particular if it is accompanied by arm-folding.

The head shrug is the position taken when one lifts the shoulders up and brings the head down low. This is another submissive stance and is sometimes a signal that one is apologetic. It says "I'm not really sure", "I'm embarrassed," or "I'm sorry."

The head nod is a universal signal that means "yes." It may be considered as a miniature bow. As we know, a bow signifies subservience. In some cultures like India and Bulgaria, signals may be confusing. Bulgarians nod to mean "no," while Indian do a kind of sideways head wobble that seems to signify disagreement. These are the exceptions, but are reasons for us to make an effort to understand cultural peculiarities. Basically, nodding indicates agreement. However, when a listener nods too rapidly, it may be a signal of impatience.

From the perspective of the person looking at or gazing at the face of another, the most neutral place to look would be the triangular area from between the eyebrows (this would be the tip of the triangle) down to the eyes and just below the nose (the base of the triangle). To look above the triangle may be perceived as intimidating and to look below it may be too intimate.

The eyes

The cliché that the eyes are the mirrors to the soul may have some truth in it. When a person is positively stimulated by what he sees, his eyes open wider, his pupils dilate, and his eyebrows are raised.

A person's pupils will dilate if he or she is excited or interested. Gazing into a person's eyes whose pupils are dilated will cause a mirroring in your own eyes and a rush of positive feelings. Bars and clubs are conducive to romance because the dim lights cause pupils to dilate, making everyone there seem more attractive.

Eyebrows that are raised make a face mimic that of a baby's and arouse protective emotions from others, especially from males toward females. This is the reason plucked eyebrows on women make them more attractive to the opposite sex. On the other hand, lowered brows show authority and seriousness.

The smile (mouth and lips)

Smiling has the same meaning all over the world. In any culture, a smile signifies happiness, friendliness and submissiveness. This is the human expression of showing non-aggression. A smile involves two groups of muscles when produced. The lower group includes the lips, cheeks and jowls, which can be controlled at will. The upper group of muscles control the eyes, producing crinkling at the corners, or "crow's feet". These are involuntary. In other words, a real smile will not only pull the outer corners of the mouth upward, but it will also involve the wrinkling around the corners of the eyes. A fake smile may look genuine at first, with the lip corners raised, but the expressionless eyes will show that it is feigned.

Showing of teeth in animals is an expression of aggression, especially if it is accompanied by the flaring of nostrils. In humans, a showing of teeth can be a sneer, and this signals anger, aggression or irritation. Look at some photos of models, actors or politicians who are supposed to be smiling. You just might discover that their smiles are actually sneers.

A person's lips are relaxed and full in their neutral state. Stress will show easily on a person's lips. Pursing indicates possible disagreement or unease towards what you are saying. When a person feels particularly stressed, angry or aggressive, he will stretch his lips until they are taut and thin. A tight-lipped smile can be a sign that the person is hiding something; he or she is not opening up completely. Lip-biting can show both interest and stress. Biting on full, relaxed lips shows interest while biting on thin, taut lips shows uneasiness or possibly repressed aggression. If a person smiles without showing the teeth, he's either faking or is self-conscious about his teeth. Looking sideways and up while smiling is said to stimulate the protective instinct, especially in males, and is found very attractive in women. Princess Diana was said to have used this kind of smile to gain sympathy, and now her sons seem to have the same smile.

Lately, the word "smize" has been coined which supposedly means "smile with the eyes." This is a word coined by Tyra Banks that refers to using the eyes rather than the lips to smile. It makes sense as, as was mentioned, true smiles are seen in the eyes. But models are now learning to fake it. Remember, you have to see an emotion expressed in different parts of the body – eyes, posture and hands, for example-before you can be certain of your body language interpretation.

Smiles stimulate a mirroring reaction that causes us to smile back. The human brain is also highly sensitive to picking up smiles, and this produces a positive response in an individual.

Arms

The chest contains the heart and lungs, vital organs in the human body. It is no wonder that, when we feel threatened, we automatically cross our arms over our chest to protect ourselves. Folding the arms over the chest is a way of making a barrier between our vital organs and whatever it is that we find threatening. This is a sign that a person feels negative about what he hears, or that he feels defensive or uneasy. Sometimes, the individual tries to relax his arms, but his legs remain crossed. Conversely, studies have shown that folding one's arms during a lecture can actually impede learning and retention of information. Intentional folding of the arms seems to signal to our brains to be cautious and skeptical about what we hear. At the same time, we send out signals to others that we are not being friendly or accommodating.

The arms are a sort of barrier for protecting vulnerable parts of the body. Men are observed to unconsciously cover their private parts when feeling insecure or dejected. Sometimes, people cross their arms and clutch at themselves to give a self-reassuring "self-hug."

The hands

Who has the "upper hand?" The phrase demonstrates how we instinctively recognize the power of the hand. Hand movements and gestures can tell you who is in power or can also help you exert influence on others. When a person is speaking, hand gestures can be considered as visual "punctuation marks," giving emphasis to their words. Of all parts of the human body, the hands are said to have the most connections with the brain.

Let's start with the palm of the hand. When we take an oath, we raise up and show the palm of our right hand. In ancient times, showing the palm revealed that one had no weapons or had laid down his weapon. Thus, showing an open palm has always been a sign of openness, honesty, and submission. A person who is trying to prove his innocence or honesty will instinctively show the palms of his hand, raising them up in front of you or holding them down at the sides of his body. A person who is hiding the truth will hide his hands from you or close his hands to hide his palms. Sometimes, the palm-hiding is subtle, as when a person pretends to have his hands busy doing something when they've been confronted. When a person puts his hands in his pockets, he is signaling his unwillingness to participate in a conversation or to open up. Holding the palm up signifies submission and holding the palm down signifies authority. When you see a couple walking hand-in-hand, you can be sure that the person with the hand on top, palm down is the one who calls the shots in the relationship. Remember Hitler's Nazi salute with the palm down?

When a person takes a palm-down hand position, with the index finger pointing and the rest curled up, it gives a threatening impression. People in authority use this gesture when scolding, reprimanding and showing displeasure. Some cultures consider this gesture extremely derogatory.

Handshakes are also a giveaway to a person's personality. It evolved from the time when men did it to prove that they carried no weapons. Now, it is a form of greeting as well as of farewell, and a way to seal an agreement.

As we have learned from the open palm, you know that the person who has his hand on top with palm down is the one who is to take the upper hand. If you find yourself shaking with your hand underneath and your palm up, you have just signified your willingness to submit. To put both hand shakers on equal footing, aim for the hands to be on the sides and the palms to be positioned vertically.

Additional gestures may accompany the handshake, like holding the elbow, arm or shoulder, or clasping the other's hand with both hands as in a sandwich. These are acceptable when there is already an existing closeness or intimacy between the two hand-shakers. If not, one may be forcing a false intimacy, and the other will feel uncomfortable and suspicious.

To get a handshake right, practice with friends or family. Wipe your hands if it's sweaty and clammy. Remember to keep you hand in a vertical position and to try to match the other's grip for a win-win handshake.

There are more interesting things that the hands can signify. When a person grasps both his hands, palm-to-palm, behind his back, he is exposing his vital organs and vulnerable organs. This is a show of confidence and courage. It is a position you will notice in policemen, royalty, your boss or other persons in authority. However, when the hands behind him show one grasping at the wrist or the upper arm, the person is exercising restraint; perhaps trying not to oppose or not to strike the other person with his other hand.

Here are other hand signals worth noting:

- Rubbing hands together - This shows expectancy or anticipation.

- Clenched hands - Shows negativity and anxiousness. The higher up the body the clenched hands are positioned, the more difficult it would be to negotiate with the person.

- The steeple- The hands face each other and index fingers are in contact. This is a gesture of confidence. Sometimes it takes a prayer-like gesture and can signify arrogance or smugness.

The thumbs

The thumbs symbolize authority, superiority and power. A showing of thumbs is a showing of confidence or a feeling of superiority. A person may tuck his hands in his front pockets with his thumbs out of the pockets. He is showing that he feels in power or superior. If he keeps his hands in his back pockets, but still with his thumbs out; he is trying to conceal his feelings of superiority. When a person points to another using his thumb, it might signal that he's about to criticize that person or that he looks down on that person. We know that crossing or folding one's arms over the chest shows resistance or disagreement. If a person has his arms crossed with his thumbs up, he is resistant and at the same time feels superior to the speaker.

The legs

We've gone through the face or head, eyes and hands. Experts have determined that the further the part of the body is from the brain, the less we are able to fake its movements. Needless to say, some people may have mastered the art of faking their face and hand movements but have absolutely no control of their leg movements. Many of us are hardly even aware of what our legs are doing while we're talking. Originally, our legs were meant to take us to our destination and to take us away from any perceived danger. To this day, and if one observes carefully, the legs always point to where the owner wants to go.

If two people are talking while standing, their legs will signal their hidden thoughts. A person who is interested or open to another will have his or her feet pointing towards the other person. Otherwise, the feet are pointing to where the owner wants to go.

As the arms are a barrier and protection for the chest, heart and lungs; the legs are a protection for the genitals. Men who stand with legs apart are showing their crotches and asserting their masculinity. Crossed legs signify the unwillingness to agree or open up. Locking ankles signifies that the person is holding back.

If during a conversation where both are seated, a man continues to bounce or jiggle one leg, he is still not completely at ease or interested. You will notice leg movements will often match with arm movements and movements of other body parts. If a person feels insecure, out-of-place or negative about a situation, he'll have his arms and legs crossed and, most likely, knitted brows. When close friends are standing or seated together, their arms and legs are open. Women, however, are trained to refrain from keeping their legs open so as not to give the wrong message. Basically, it's best to keep the knees together. Having both legs straight and side-by-side shows neutrality.

The voice

It sounds unfair but, more often than not, people respond more to a person's voice than to what they are saying. A person's voice is the result of how he feels inside. Intelligence agents are said to be able to detect deception from a person's voice, specifically from a change in pitch. If you are insecure or nervous, it will be all too evident in your voice.

Most people respond most positively to a well-modulated and soothing voice. We find it easy to guess a person's emotions from the voice – we can tell if a person is intimidated, excited, confident or nervous. Unfortunately, our voices may have natural qualities that can give the wrong impression. A naturally high-pitched voice, for example, might make people perceive the speaker as nervous or a nagger. A present voice fad called "vocal fry" is becoming popular among young women. Britney Spears is said to possess this kind of voice. It involves speaking with a low but screechy tone and ending sentences with a rise in tone as if asking a question. Women who speak this way, unfortunately, are perceived to be unprofessional and less trustworthy. Equally unfortunate is that statements made by people with accents are often also highly doubted or considered dishonest. The brain's difficulty in processing words uttered with an accent presumably makes people find difficulty believing what they hear.

The tone, volume and pacing of the voice is greatly influenced by one's health so taking good care of your health and your vocal apparatus will be a great help in giving the right impression using your voice.

Chapter 3

Body Language in the

Workplace

After the last chapter, hopefully you're feeling a bit more knowledgeable when it comes to reading other people via their body language. You now have the understanding necessary to be able to start discerning what your students or potential clients may be thinking. But what's more amazing is how you can use your knowledge of body language to benefit yourself directly.

Did you know that, by intentionally assuming positive poses or making positive actions or gestures, you can fool your brain into believing that you are indeed positive, indeed confident and indeed happy? This is very exciting because it gives us more control over our feelings and makes it easier for us to remain optimistic and find success in what we do. Some people see it as faking, but if you do it often enough, you can re-wire your brain and genuinely be more confident, assertive, happy or whatever it is that you aim to be. We can adjust our mood by doing things in reverse - do the action to make the mind feel the emotion. So, while you may have been thinking that your ability to read body language has given you the power to "read" minds, what you may not have realized is that understanding body language gives you the power to make powerful changes in your own life!

Getting that job

You've polished your resume, and you've got your best business suit ready. Remember, your actions can tell the interviewer more than your words or your resume. Your goal in an interview is to appear professional, reliable, open, honest, and responsible. You may feel nervous, but you also want to put the interviewer at ease and show that you can fit comfortably into their work environment.

It starts even before the interview

The use of proper body language starts with the receptionist. Many interviewers ask the receptionist for feedback on your attitude and behavior. Assume that the person walking with you to the elevator might be your interviewer or future boss, never take anything or anyone for granted.

I know someone who joined a talent contest. On the way there, the person walking ahead of her was blocking her path. She and her friends rudely made caustic remarks about how slowly that person was walking as they passed by. Imagine her chagrin when, during the contest, the "slow poke" turned out to be one of the judges. Even before the actual interview, be aware that you may already be under evaluation.

Be open

Avoid making barriers between you and the interviewer. Sit up straight, showing your neck, chest and stomach area. You may not feel confident enough to do this but try it. Remember, do the actions and your brain will follow suit. Do not cross your arms over your chest, keep your hands lightly clenched on your lap or the desk. Keep your lap free and put your bag on the floor, if necessary. Do not slouch or look too relaxed. You might give the impression that you are lazy or arrogant.

Give a good handshake

In this case, you want to acknowledge the interviewer's authority, so feel free to offer your hand with the palm slightly up if you feel it's necessary. Allow the interviewer to take a slightly dominant position in the handshake if they try. This will make the interviewer see you as a person who will not be difficult to work with. Take your cue from the interviewer and follow the strength of his or her grip. Mimicry will also give a good impression. Follow the interviewer's pace and stride as you're led to your seat.

Respect personal space

If you're not sure, wait for the interviewer to indicate where you should sit. I necessary, ask where you may sit. Sitting in the interviewer's space is obviously a big no-no. Leaning slightly forward can indicate interest, but leaning too far forward may cause you to invade the interviewer's personal space.

Allow a twenty-second size up

Before you move on to the next tip, take a few seconds to allow the interviewer to size you up. This is entirely subconscious and natural. People typically need about 20 seconds to note everything about you from head to foot and to store information they will also refer to (again subconsciously) in making their overall assessment of you. You may simply sit and prepare your documents to allow this to happen.

When this is not done, tension can develop as the interviewer may not be able to concentrate and note what you say during the interview. This is an important 20 seconds that will significantly influence the outcome of your interview. This is not the same as being checked out. This is just a natural part of our process of taking stock of others.

Make eye contact

As mentioned earlier in this book, imagine a triangle with its point between the interviewer's eyebrows and the two corners at the corners of the eyes. The base of this imaginary triangle should be above the lips. Focus on this triangle to show interest. Blink occasionally in order not to stare awkwardly. This will demonstrate that you are interested and trustworthy. Be careful not to gaze below the imaginary triangle as this could give a different meaning.

Make open palm gestures

While speaking, use your hands to articulate your ideas. Use open palm gestures and keep your hands below your face and above your waist (make sure your hands can be seen). The open palms indicate that you are knowledgeable and willing to use what you know to help the company.

Show interest with your legs

Keep both feet on the floor, pointing towards the interviewer. Avoid unnecessary and repetitive leg movements like shaking and jiggling as this could signal boredom and disinterest. Women wearing skirts can appear more businesslike if they simply keep their knees together and avoid crossing their legs. Crossed legs can be acceptable as it signals submissiveness. It is especially important not to pair crossed legs with crossed arms as this would indicate an overall negative viewpoint or unwillingness to communicate.

Make a graceful exit

Rise as smoothly as possible, smile, nod and thank the interviewer. Make as smooth an exit as possible.

At a business meeting or making a presentation

Business meetings may involve people you already work with or people you've just met whom you might need to sign a deal with. If the meeting is with people you're meeting for the first time and have to impress, most of the body language for a job interview would also apply. Here are more tips that will also work when dealing with co-workers.

It's important to try to gauge how the person you're talking to is feeling. Take a look at the individual's eyes. If they're downcast, and the person is seemingly avoiding you, then something has to be worked out. Other signs of defensiveness, conflict in points of view or unwillingness to cooperate are arms folded across chest, the whole body facing away from you, feet facing away or towards the exit, and absence of open gestures. Watch also for pursed or tight lips and arms tightly grasped. Frequent blinking and eyes darting from side to side also signify boredom and a desire to find a way out. Your sensitivity to these signals will help you respond in a way that will help ease the tension and make the others more receptive and agreeable.

It's best to be prepared for business meetings, not only in terms of what is going to be discussed but also in terms of how you can present yourself in such a way that will assure successful communication and negotiation.

Food and drink

You may know all the right moves, all the ways to project yourself positively, but some other factors could affect your body language and emphasize the negative. Being hungry could make you grumpy and impatient, and that will show quickly in your body language. If you've drunk too much coffee, it will also show. The basics of being mindful of what you eat and drink still apply here. Imagine how people will respond to you if you come off as highly-strung and impatient.

Be prepared

These are things that you can do before facing everyone else, to prep you to make a good impression. It is important to have all the data or all the information you'll need to persuade, convince, present or defend, or whatever the purpose of the meeting will be. Not knowing the facts or the background about what you have to discuss will leave you groping or bluffing and this will come out in your body language.

Stand tall with your feet apart, exposing your neck, chest and stomach areas. Put your hands on your hips to appear bigger than you are. This is a power pose. Even if you don't feel powerful or confident, assuming such a pose sends a message to your brain to release more testosterone that *will* make you truly confident. Power positions are assumed when you take up more space. You can also use the palms down position to show authority. Lay your hands on the table as you assume your power pose. Appearing more confident will make people listen and believe in what you say. Remember that this is best done before you stand in front of everyone, to rev up the power hormones and give you a boost of confidence. Depending on the situation, when you do present yourself, you may have to take a more friendly-looking stance. Be confident but not too aggressive.

If you've been under a lot of stress before the meeting, be aware that your face may be "set" in its stressed, sad or perplexed state. Facing a mirror and smiling at yourself can erase the negative expression on your face and trigger reactions in your body and brain that will make you feel happier and more confident.

Listen

Whether you're the boss or subordinate, it always helps to use body language that shows that you are listening and that you value what the other person is saying. This requires eye contact, nodding, as well as open arm and leg movements. Touch a closed hand to your chin or cheek, with your index finger pointing towards your forehead to show that you are digesting and evaluating what you hear. Resting your head on your hand will indicate boredom, however. Simply tilting your head a bit to the side will signal to the speaker that you are listening and interested.

Put the phone aside

Studies have shown that using small gadgets before giving a presentation can make a person less assertive. Larger contraptions like desktops or laptops encourage more confidence because their larger size encourages more open movements.

Use a pen or pointer

A big chunk of the information people process comes from what they see. Using a pen or pointer to direct the listener's gaze to the information you are describing reinforces his perception of it. After introducing the information visually as well as verbally, subtly bringing the pointer or pen to the level of your eyes will bring the listener's gaze you yours, making a powerful impact and ensuring that the information is clearly embedded in the listener's mind. Using open palm gestures while doing this and explaining will make this a positive experience for the listener.

Influencing people

Knowing about body language and the "power" that comes with it can be dangerous if used in the wrong way. With body language, you can dominate or manipulate a person. But this is not our purpose in influencing. The purpose of using body language to influence is to establish an environment that will make others comfortable, more cooperative and willing to contribute their skills, talents or other resources in order to achieve a common goal.

Nod

Nodding encourages a person to trust and to open up because it signals your agreement, understanding and non-aggression. If you nod to show agreement, the other person relaxes, loses any aggression he may harbor and begins to trust in you. Just like yawning, nodding is also contagious. As your nod your head, the listener will unconsciously find himself nodding as well and becoming more open to your ideas.

Show your openness

Use open palms, tilted head, eye contact, smiling and legs pointed toward the person to signal "I am with you." This will make the person more willing to work with you.

Do some mirroring

People who are close to each other, like married couples, begin to resemble each other because of mirroring, this is the tendency to copy or imitate a person's body language. This is normally subconscious and is part of our programming in order to survive. This was said to have started in the womb where the fetus learned to match the rhythms of its mother's womb. It may also be a primitive survival tactic, when being different or not belonging could have cost an individual his life. Although this occurs naturally when people spend time together and share common goals or beliefs, a little conscious mirroring can send signals to the other person that you have similar goals and that you support each other.

Enlarge your space

Open up and expose your neck, chest, and stomach. Stand straight and tall, with your arms on your hips to appear bigger. You will be perceived as confident and authoritative, and you will feel bolder as well.

Use touch

Light brushing of the hand or shoulder can give a "personal touch." Give a friendly pat on the shoulder, for example. A study showed that salespeople who lightly brushed the fingers of their clients while handing them their change were perceived as having better personal skills than those who didn't. Other similar studies gave similar results, with overall positive views towards the "touchers." Waiters who touched were also reportedly given larger tips. A three-second touch on the elbow (not above or below) can produce positive results. Be careful, however, to consider the cultural context. Remember to respect personal space as well.

Smile

The human brain has been wired in such a way that people automatically respond to a smile. A sincere smile can automatically diffuse tension and resistance. Using humor will automatically break barriers in communication.

Tell the tale

Using hand gestures while explaining or giving instructions is almost as good as using visual aids. People are visually oriented, and hand movements help them to retain information given verbally as the hands are acting out the words. But keep your hands below your face, holding the hands too high up is perceived as less powerful.

Use a convincing voice

People are convinced more by their impression of you than by the facts you may be presenting them with. A deep and smooth voice is said to be pleasant and more convincing to the listener. It means that one must be reasonably relaxed and composed in order to produce this kind of voice. Humming can help warm up your voice before speaking.

Take a good look

Some people are not so good at picking up subtle signs, so you have to make more assertive signals. If you're the boss or a person who's supposed to be in charge, there will be times when you'll have to take an extra step to make this felt. Imagine that a person has a "third eye" on his forehead just slightly above and between the eyebrows, sort of like a Cyclops. Turn your gaze on that third eye and don't go down. This is a power gaze that works well on particularly belligerent subordinates. Narrowing your eyelids and not blinking will make this look more intimidating.

Use makeup and wear eyeglasses

If you're a woman, wearing makeup will make people perceive you to be more competent and intelligent. This has been observed to be especially so when wearing glasses. Wearing light-colored lipstick makes you more credible in a business setting (save your hot-red lipstick for a date).

Be clever

You may think of it as a game, and a little one-upmanship could help. To prevent people from assuming closed positions (crossing legs and arms) while you speak, hand out pens, handouts or illustrations to help the audience keep their arms open and occupied. If are small in stature and someone is trying to intimidate you with their size or position, you can make him sit in a chair lower than yours or, if he's sitting in a power pose, stand up to offset this.

Signal that the conversation is over

Doctor's are trained to show that a session has gone on for too long unnecessarily by sitting back and cutting off eye contact. You can do the same or turn your body slightly away from the other person to signal that you have to get back to work. This usually works although you may have to say outright that you have to get back to work if the other person hasn't picked up on your signals.

Make a power exit

It's not over until you're outside of the door. Be aware that people will be looking at your back as you leave, so make sure it will give the right impression. There shouldn't be any thread hanging from the hemline of your clothing and your shoes should be shined at the back. Look back just before you step out, smile and close the door behind you. People's last memory of you before you step out should be of you smiling.

Chapter 4

Body Language in your

Personal Life

The great thing about understanding how the body sends signals is that you can use what you know to improve your relationship with family and friends as well establish new ones. It's like a shortcut to creating an immediate bond and rapport. Some of the gestures here have the same meaning in the workplace but are re-introduced (at the risk of being redundant) to emphasize how they are used in a different setting.

Showing interest and enhancing communication

A person will immediately find you likable if you send them the right signals. However, sending the right signals not only makes you likable, but it also makes the other person less defensive and more at ease. Establishing rapport makes it easier for both sides to be their true selves. The techniques are still the same and we will go through them more briefly.

Use open signals

Again, as we've discussed in Chapters 2 and 3, opening up shows that we are honest, willing to listen, interested and non-threatening. Smile, tilt your head, raise your eyebrows, show the palms of your hand, lean a little bit forward and do not cross your arms or your legs.

Mirror, mirror

Mirroring says "we are like-minded." This is the shortcut to establishing and bond with a person. If you sense that someone feels nervous around you, mirroring can help put him at ease. Of course, keep it subtle and you shouldn't mirror the negatives.

Nod to persuade

Nodding shows agreement and interest. It is also contagious and the other person will find himself nodding and feeling more agreeable to what you are saying.

Stroke your chin

We do this unconsciously but you can also use this to intentionally encourage the person to keep talking.

Ready and set

If you're the speaker, you might see the other person leaning slightly forward with one foot forward and hands grasping the sides of the seat as if ready to leave. It could mean two things - he's ready to leave because he doesn't agree with you or he's ready to take what you said to action. You'll have to check for other signals to know what it means. If you noticed negative signals before this, then you'll have to take a different approach to what you are saying.

Pace yourself

Have you ever noticed how, when you're having a conversation with someone with an accent, you find yourself gradually acquiring the accent as your conversation goes along? This is an example of *pacing*. It is mirroring the way a person speaks. To build rapport and enhance communication, try to keep with the other person's pace. Speaking too fast will make the other person feel tense and under pressure. Try to mirror the other person's intonation, inflection and speaking speed. This can help you achieve especially good results when setting appointments on the phone.

Make the right approach

You may be giving open signals which are positive, but if you approach too directly, you may be perceived as being aggressive. An approach from the side is less threatening. Women, whether consciously or unconsciously, fear being attacked from behind, so approach at an angle from the front. Men fear a frontal attack so approach at an angle from the rear or side.

Parenting

Children are naturally adept at reading body language because their brains are programmed to learn from the actions of people around them. Parents have to make sure they're sending the right signals to their kids. As children grow older, they can be taught more about body language, including how to use it to send out positive messages and how to improve their connections with others. Children nowadays do a lot of "socializing" on the internet, and this may make them less adept at understanding and using body language in face-to-face encounters; so it's important for parents to inform them about its value in their lives.

Be consistent

"Don't touch that," you yell, with a grin. You're stating a rule, but your smile says you're not serious. Your child will most probably ignore the rule. It's best to assume a neutral face.

A request is not a question

When it's time for bed, it's time for bed. If you say it with an inflection at the end, you make it a question, and you are giving your child the option to follow or not to follow.

Actions speak louder than hurtful words

You may not verbalize it, but your body language is saying it loud and clear. Avoid signals that give negative messages like eye-rolling, arm-crossing or ignoring your child while fiddling with your phone or tablet.

Train by example

Many times, the lessons you instill most successfully in your children are the ones that you model through your actions. They may not listen when you ask them to clean their rooms now, but if you set an example of keeping things neat, they're likely to show the same regard for neatness when they're older.

Where is the love?

Remember that your children are not your co-workers or subordinates. Show that you love them by speaking in a low, soothing voice; sit beside them and gaze at them lovingly as you listen to their stories. Showing them positive body signals will help them grow up into competent and confident adults.

When they are made to feel uncomfortable

Teach your children to resist and to tell you if anyone's body language towards them is making them feel uncomfortable. Let them know that they have the right not to accept it if anybody looks at them or acts in any way that makes them feel uneasy.

Dating

What the signs that your date is into you? Below, we'll take a look at the signs that your date is or isn't interested in you, broken down by gender.

Men and women

Raising the eyebrows - This is a universal sign of interest. It's like an unspoken hello.

Dilated pupils - Increased interest and brain activity cause the pupils to dilate. Gazing into another person's eyes whose pupils are dilated will also cause your eyes to dilate. Dim lights make the eyes widen and may cause couples to feel more romantic. Some women wear contact lenses that make the eyes appear to have dilated pupils because it makes them look more attractive. Advertisers often photoshop eyes of models in pictures to make the eyes look dilated.

Mirroring - When a person is into you, he or she will unconsciously copy your movements.

Pointing the feet or legs towards you - People are not usually aware of this, but their feet will point towards a person they like or the place where they'd like to go. Their knees will also do the same.

Leaning forward - They want to hear you better, they want to get closer, and they want to show that they're interested.

Women

If only men were more attentive, they would be able to respond more effectively to the many signs a woman makes to show that she's interested. Pay attention gentlemen!

Preening - Watch for the many ways she'll make herself more attractive to you. She'll fix her hair, straighten her dress, adjust her jewelry, moisten her lips, emphasize her curves and cross her legs to make them look longer.

The face platter - She rests both elbows on the table and puts one hand over the other under her chin, presenting her face as though on a platter.

Wrist display - She will show the delicate skin or her inner wrists in many ways., for example, when flicking her hair, raising her cigarette, or letting you smell her perfume.

Releasing pheromones - Tossing or flicking hair or subtly raising her arms to expose the armpits are her way of releasing pheromones.

Touching - Light accidental or intentional touches are a sign that she's interested.

Access to her purse - Her bag or purse is almost like an extension of her body. Placing it close to you or allowing you access to its contents is a signal that she likes you.

Men

Preening - He will smoothen his shirt, fix his tie, adjust his watch or cufflinks, run his fingers through his hair and perform other grooming activities to look attractive.

Dishevelment - He may leave his tie or his collar askew to make you fix it for him.

Talk - Men know that women like to speak, and they willingly engage in getting-to know-you conversation to encourage a woman to feel more open and comfortable with him. This talk, however, may soon dry up as soon as he knows you're his.

Highlights his asset - Unconsciously, he will emphasize his male parts by sitting with his legs slightly spread out, putting his hands in his pockets with his thumbs pointing towards the groin, or adjusting his belt.

Catches his breath - As he breathes in deeply, he puffs up his chest and narrows his waist. These are traits women have unconsciously learned, since prehistoric times, to consider desirable because they show his ability to defend and protect.

Detecting lies and deception

Detecting lying and deception may not be that easy. Experts in body language use videos and watch over and over to catch those fleeting tell-tale movements that give away that a person has lied. Seasoned liars are also masters of body language, and they know how to act as if they are telling the truth. It is commonly said that liars cannot look you in the eye, but the fact is they DO look you in the eye, and even more so than a person who's telling the truth. Lying causes nervousness and stress that a liar may be able to mask. But chemicals in the body cause some irritation or changes around the face and neck that bring about some tell-tale gestures. Depending on how skillful the liar is, the gesture may be overt or extremely fleeting and subtle. Look out for the following:

- Scratching or touching the nose

- Covering the mouth or touching a finger to the mouth

- Touching or covering an ear

- Adjusting one's shirt collar

- Scratching the neck

- Rubbing an eye

- Swallowing hard and several times

- Blinking rapidly

These mannerisms are said to be done while the person is telling the lie. But remember, body language is not a "one size fits all" kind of thing, so be careful before you arrive at a hasty conclusion. That man may be scratching his nose and rubbing his eyes because he has an allergy.

Avoiding possible harm, abuse or threats to your life

This could be one of the most important reasons for understanding body language. It could save your life. It may not always be possible to accurately interpret another person's body language, but being aware and alert could make a big difference.

Defensive body language to diffuse (minor) aggression

When a person in authority seems to be in a rage because of a mistake you have committed, assume a defensive stance. You could make yourself appear smaller by bowing your head, tucking your chin in, crossing your arms and locking your ankles together. This may douse the person's aggression.

Preventing a possible attack on the street

I once heard a mugger confess to reporters that his most likely victim would be someone who looked lost and insecure rather than someone who looked confident and aware of what was happening around him. When walking down the street, make big strides, swing your arms at your sides and hold your head up. Make eye contact with people walking towards you. Thieves do not want people to note their features. Their more likely victims are people looking down while walking and who are unaware of the people around them. Be aware of people who seem to be distracting you in some way- by yelling suddenly and loudly, touching you on the left side of your body (to steal your valuables on your right), suddenly and seemingly innocently blocking your path, asking impertinent questions, etc. These may all be tactics to divert your attention while they divest you of your valuables.

Detecting a possibly abusive person

Abusive individuals can seem charming, effusive in their flattery and generous with their gifts at first but don't be fooled. Take note of these signs of a potential abuser:

- Makes gestures that make him appear bigger than he is - standing tall, legs apart, arms on hips

- Feeling of entitlement, disregard of rules because he believes he is above it; will not wait in line or for his turn, for example

- Rude behavior (shouting or swearing, mocking, belittling) toward people he considers inferior like the waiter or taxi driver, a disabled individual or an individual of another race.

- Showing disinterest when you talk about yourself; looking away, turning body away from you or towards the exit, rolling eyes, frowning, crossing arms, etc.

- When angry, makes threatening gestures like shaking of fists, punching objects, poking object of anger with his finger, breaking things, etc. Face may be flushed with anger and voice may be inappropriately loud

- Antisocial and aloof behavior

Signs that you should consider getting out of a relationship

If during an argument, the other person becomes flushed with anger, begins to sweat, clenches his jaw and fists, points his index finger angrily or pokes you,

you could become a victim of violence, and you should get out of the situation.

Suspicious behavior in public places (grocery stores, airports, bus and train stations, etc.) and public transport

If you detect suspicious behavior, consider moving away or alerting security. Of course, it's important to use your judgement and not jump to conclusions. However, as the saying goes, better safe than sorry!

- Wearing clothing inappropriate for the weather (like a coat on a scorching day)

- Nervousness, trembling, fidgeting, rubbing hands, breathing heavily, pacing and sweating

- Making diagrams, taking photos of infrastructure, not availing of services (loitering), suddenly leaving when approached or noticed

- Having a trance-like or dazed expression

- Repeated patting of the front or upper part of the body (may signify carrying of weapon)

- Showing exaggerated or extreme emotions; crying and then suddenly laughing

All this may sound frightening, but most survivors of violent attacks are those who kept alert and were mindful of what was happening around them.

Chapter 5

Body Language Across Cultures

I'm sure that you've already learned a lot from the previous chapters, and you may feel you're on the way to becoming a body language expert. This last chapter will help you make sure that no misunderstandings arise because of cultural differences, and is a reminder that we have to consider the differences across cultures and individuals. Moreover, this chapter may save you the embarrassment (or worse) of committing a cultural faux pas.

The Handshake

Surprisingly, handshakes tend to be done more frequently in other parts of the world than in the United States. The handshake is now recognized worldwide as a standard gesture in business as well as social meetings, but there are still some variations. In Muslim countries for instance, members of the opposite sex cannot shake hands, as it's taboo. An Orthodox Jew, who is male, will also likely not shake hands with a woman.

Asia

East Asian countries usually bow instead of shaking hands. Globalization, however, has made the handshake acceptable as well. But do not expect a strong handshake. Asian handshakes may be limp, especially between members of the opposite sex. The Thais, Vietnamese and Laotians make a small bow with hands together in front as if in prayer, called a *wai*. Indians put their hands together to *Namaste*. When in Russia, never shake over a threshold because it is believed to result in disagreement.

Africa

In South Africa, handshakes are expected to be strong.

Europe

People in Europe often shake hands whenever they meet, not only at the beginning or end of a meeting. In

Belgium, unwillingness to shake hands may give the impression that you're untrustworthy and snobbish. In France, handshakes tend to be firm and quick. Germans also tend to give a quick pump. After a business meeting, they may consider you familiar enough to bid farewell with air kisses on both cheeks. The English generally give more pumps than the Germans when they shake hands, but as a rule, Americans tend to give the most pumps. Receiving more or less pumps than one is used to could make one assume the giver as either too enthusiastic or somewhat indifferent.

South America

Most South American countries accept light kisses on one or both cheeks.

Personal distance

The zones that you are allowed to enter into around an individual varies from country to country. In Italy and Japan, for example, you are often allowed to get as close as 10 inches to a person. Australians and Americans, however, will allow you to stand not closer than 18 inches. Encroaching on someone's intimate zone may be misconstrued as being pushy, or worse, sexual harassment. Not allowing someone to get closer, however, will be seen as aloofness. Personal distance is not the same as bodily contact or touching. Although the Japanese will allow you to stand close to them, any physical contact would generally be considered impolite.

The head

In most Asian countries, the head is considered sacred and should not be touched. Parents are appalled when foreigners pat their children on the head.

Saying yes

Nodding is usually an indication of agreement. However, in Greece, Bulgaria, Yugoslavia, and Turkey, nodding means *no*.

The head wobble that looks more like a head shake is common in India, and it could mean either yes or no. Indians wobble their heads to express understanding or agreement; or to mean no when they'd rather not say it.

To the Japanese, *hai* is translated as yes but they may say it simply to mean "go on" or "keep talking," even though they disagree. In general, most Westerners are direct with their answers while Asians will let you know through context. You will have to pick up clues from other information they give you. This may be bewildering to some or even annoying, but respecting the long-held beliefs and understanding the psyche of a collective culture will help you adjust accordingly and communicate more efficiently.

Smiling and display of emotions

Compared to the more openly expressive West; in the East, overly open displays of emotion are usually avoided so as not to disrupt the status quo. Smiling is done to keep the harmony and is not necessarily a show of happiness. It can be used to mask embarrassment, loss of face, fear, shyness, confusion, annoyance or simply being at a loss for words.

Eye contact

In most parts of Africa and Asia, prolonged eye contact is considered rude and an expression of defiance. Looking down is considered as a sign of humility and respect. In Japan, a listening audience may keep their eyes closed to shut out distractions and to focus on the speaker's words.

The nose, having a cold, handkerchiefs and spitting

Tapping the nose may be done intentionally to convey a message. In England it means "confidential;" in Italy, it's a warning to watch out.

Usually, in Asia, a cold is thought to be better dealt with loud snorting and spitting. Westerners would prefer to blow their noses. Handkerchiefs are not popular in Asia as it is unthinkable to use them and carrying them around, harboring germs. In Philippine history, handkerchiefs used to play a part in courtship rituals, but are now simply carried around by some ladies for the purpose of filtering out polluted air and wiping away sweat.

The mouth and kissing

In the West, kissing in public is accepted and when kissing the cheeks, can be a form of greeting or display or affection. Most Asians are not as open to this, whether for religious or cultural reasons. Avoid trying to kiss anyone of the opposite sex or on the first introduction. In the Middle East, kissing is a standard greeting, but not with the opposite sex. In Native American, Filipino and Latin American countries, people often use their mouths to point, rather than their forefingers.

More about hands

In most of Asia, the left and right hands are not equal in status. The left hand is considered the "dirty hand."

To be safe, always use the right hand. Business cards or anything handed to you should be received using the right hand. Conservative businessmen in East Asia will hand you their business cards with both hands and a bow. It is polite to accept in a similar fashion.

The "OK" sign, made using the thumb and forefinger is recognized all over the world. There are some differences to be noted, however. In France, it means "zero." In Japan, it means "money." As for Turkey, Greece and most of Latin America, it is an obscenity.

The "victory sign" using the fore and middle fingers is recognized in The US and some parts of Europe. If you do this sign with the back of your hand facing the other person (palm facing-in), it will be taken as an obscenity or an insult in the UK, Australia and New Zealand.

Thanks to Facebook, the thumbs-up sign (the 'like' emoticon) is beginning to have universal acceptance. For some countries though, such as Greece, it is another obscenity. Remember that the thumb is a symbol of power and superiority. Thrusting your thumb up sharply can be demeaning.

The "rock 'n roll sign" or the sign or the horns, using the forefinger and little finger, is commonly made at rock concerts or by fans of the Texas Longhorns. Be careful, because in Italy this sign is an insult to a man's wife.

Legs and feet

Leg-crossing is acceptable in North America and Europe. In Asia and the Middle East, it may be considered rude. Many East Asian cultures also believe the showing of the soles of the feet or shoes to be very disrespectful.

Our world is so diverse, and striving to act appropriately seems so challenging. Most cultures are forgiving and understanding when foreigners commit mistakes. Perhaps the best thing to do is to ask the locals what is and isn't acceptable so that you can behave accordingly.

Conclusion

As you have no doubt seen, there are many factors involved when it comes to body language, and that it is not always easy to accurately interpret the meaning which lies behind the body language of others. You may be wondering how it would ever be possible to remember everything you've read, but the truth is, there is still so much to learn.

By following the guidelines outlined in this book, you will be well on your way to understanding the true thoughts and feelings of others, beyond what they are saying. In addition, with a little practice you'll soon be on your way to making your body language work for you , which in turn will allow you to connect better with others and give a much better account of yourself. The key is sensitivity; be observant and you will soon develop the instinct to pick up signals and respond accordingly.

Good luck!

A message from the author, Steve Gold

Be sure to check out my other books. Check the back of this book for a list of other books written by me.

Finally, if you enjoyed this book, **please** take the time to post a review on Amazon. It will only take a couple of minutes and I'd be extremely grateful for your support.

Thank you again for your support.

Steve Gold

FREE BONUS!: Preview Of

"Interview - How To Best Prepare For An Interview And Land Your Dream Job"!

If you enjoyed this book, I have a little bonus for you; a preview of one of my other books ""Interview - How To Best Prepare For An Interview And Land Your Dream Job In 2016!"". In this book, we'll take a closer look at exactly what employers are looking for from interviewees, and how best to prepare for an interview so as to give yourself the best chance of landing your dream job!

Introduction

It is not too much of an exaggeration to think of a job interview as one of the most nerve wrecking situations one can be in. For young job seekers just starting off, it can be a defining moment which – whatever the outcome may be – can have a massive impact on one's self-esteem. For career changers, there's no telling what to expect in the unpredictable job market.

Times have certainly changed, and so have the requirements and expectations of employers; what was acceptable or applicable a few years ago may not be so in the modern age. This also means that hiring practices are no longer the same. Ultimately, when it comes to nailing a job interview, knowledge is power and preparation is key – that will never change. The question then becomes how can one adapt to changing hiring practices and ace a job interview in the current climate? What are the things one should know and how can one be best prepared?

In the following chapters, you will gain a better understanding of the job interview process as well as common interviewing practices that are unique to this particular period in time. You will then be guided on how to best prepare when called for a job interview, from what questions to anticipate and how to best handle the tricky ones in order to give yourself the best possible chance of landing the job. Insights will also begin on making a good first impression the moment you meet the hiring manager.

Getting called for an interview is a golden opportunity afforded only to a handful of hopefuls who apply for a job opening, so you need to make the most out of it.

Good luck!

Chapter 1

The Job Interview Demystified

After sending out numerous job applications and patiently waiting, you've finally got the much anticipated call to go for an interview with a potential employer. Having managed to get a job interview means you have surpassed countless other applicants vying for the job, and are among the shortlisted candidates deemed qualified to fill the position. You are being given the chance to convince a potential employer firsthand that you are the person their organization needs. As such, you want to be sure to make the most out of this golden opportunity by putting your best foot forward and, hopefully, secure the job you want.

Job Interviews: Then vs. Now

In the not-so-distant past, people were oftentimes introduced to job openings through being referred by someone or by browsing the classified advertisements in newspapers. Competition was not as though, and if you were lucky enough to be referred by someone the employer knew and trusted, you were likely to already have an advantage over the other candidates.

However, when the internet became the main outlet for recruitment and job searching in the new millennium, it changed the game. Job applicants began to have easier access to information on who was hiring, leading to a significantly higher responses to job postings. Recruiters were then faced with the overwhelming task of sorting through hundreds, maybe even thousands, of applications and narrowing down potential candidates to a small handful. The selected few would then have to go through a tough interview process until the suitable candidate was found from among the hopefuls.

It is hardly a surprise that recruiters have changed their interviewing practices, and now take a tougher approach when screening for suitable candidates. Thus, job seekers now have additional criteria to fulfill in addition to simply stating their credentials, if they want to land that dream job in todays increasingly competitive environment.

What a Recruiter Wants

A job interview is a twofold process. On one hand, a potential employer will be gauging whether you have the capacity to competently fulfill the required role. The interview also allows for a company to form a well-rounded impression of whether a candidate has the personality and motivation to succeed in the particular industry for which they are interviewing. On the other hand, an interviewee has the opportunity to assess whether joining the organization is in line with their career goals, and is also given the chance to convince the hiring manager as to why they are the right fit for a job opening.

Perhaps the most baffling aspect of job hunting is figuring out exactly what recruiters are looking for. More importantly though, how can one get ahead of the pack to become that one outstanding candidate from many who actually lands the job?

The profile of an ideal employee differs from employer to employer. However, the basic tenets of having integrity, the drive to excel and the ability to learn quickly will generally get one noticed, especially if one has ambitions of climbing the corporate ladder. Even though there is no doubt that hard work, perseverance and diligence are essential qualities for success in any job, there are qualities outside of credentials and experience that will get the attention of employers – namely, attitude and mindset.

Businesses are facing various intense challenges in the current economy and market place. This increased competition has meant that companies now need to be lean and efficient. Thus, oftentimes they need employees who can do more than simply perform one particular function in the company. Favorable candidates are the ones who demonstrate creativity, commitment and passion to the job, showing that they are adaptable in a fast-paced working environment and are able to contribute to the business growth agenda in the industry for the long-run.

In summation, as a job seeker, your career survival and progression depends on how much you can contribute to an organization besides what is already specifically requested in the job description. The job interview is a window of opportunity in which you should be aiming to convince a potential employer that, not only can you fulfill the job requirements, but you can bring more to the table than what is being requested.

Check out the rest of "Interview - How To Best Prepare For An Interview And Land Your Dream Job!" on Amazon.

Check Out My Other Books!

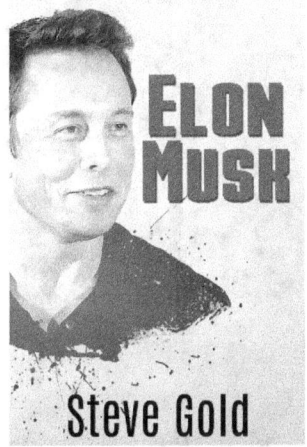

Elon Musk - The Biography Of A Modern Day Renaissance Man

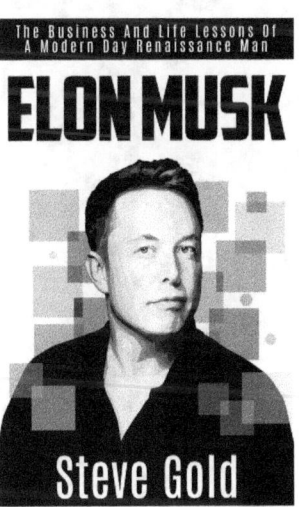

Elon Musk - The Business & Life Lessons Of A Modern Day Renaissance Man

Warren Buffett - The Business And Life Lessons Of An Investment Genius, Magnate And Philanthropist

Steve Jobs - The Biography & Lessons Of The Mastermind Behind Apple

Management - Achieve Management Excellence & World Class Leadership Skills In 7 Simple Steps

Sales - Easily Sell Anything To Anyone & Achieve Sales Excellence In 7 Simple Steps

Arduino - Getting Started With Arduino: The Ultimate Beginner's Guide

(If the links do not work, for whatever reason, you can simply search for these titles on the Amazon to find them. All books available as ebooks or printed books)

www.ingramcontent.com/pod-product-compliance
Lightning Source LLC
Chambersburg PA
CBHW071407280526
45787CB00001B/477